Dedicated to the hopes and dreams of children everywhere.

ISBN # 978-0-9965956-6-7

Contact us at:

DantheFish9@gmail.com

Jonathan the Porcupine

By Cathie Gebhart and Jonathan Antoine

Illustrated by Chelsea Rae Meeker

Once there was a porcupine named Jonathan. He was a happy little porcupine who loved to sing. He sang in the sunshine and sang in the moonlight. He sang in the house and sang in the garden. Singing made Jonathan's heart soar.

As Jonathan grew, he realized he did not look the same as the other animals at school. The rabbits looked soft and lovely. The chipmunks looked small and cute. The squirrels had fabulous bushy tails. But Jonathan had sharp-looking quills, a long pointy nose, and beady eyes.

No one thought he was lovely or cute or even like someone they wanted as a friend. The other animals would avoid him, and some made fun of him. The squirrels were the worst. They called him all sorts of names.

The names hurt Jonathan, and he became very quiet. He was hoping if he was quiet enough, everyone would stop noticing him and stop calling him names. Soon, the other animals forgot he was even there.

His teachers forgot, too. Jonathan felt invisible, but safe. It was very lonely to be invisible.

Jonathan still had music in his heart, but he kept it quiet and no longer sang to the sun or the moon. Jonathan thought the sun and the moon probably forgot he was there, too.

One day, Jonathan's grandmother called and wanted to see him. Jonathan quietly trudged down the street to his grandmother's house. He kept his eyes fixed on the ground to avoid seeing the animals playing outside, and he hoped they didn't see him.

His grandmother opened the door and gave him a hug. She always knew he was there, no matter how quiet he tried to be.

"There is someone I want you to meet," his grandmother said, taking Jonathan into the house. "This is my friend, Mrs. Hedgehog. She teaches people to sing."

"You can call me Mrs. H," she said to Jonathan. "Nice to meet you."

Jonathan didn't look up, but wondered why a singing teacher was at his grandmother's house.

Mrs. H sat down at his grandmother's piano and started to play. The song was so beautiful that Jonathan felt happy for the first time in a long time.

Then Mrs. H started to sing. Jonathan looked up from the ground to watch and listen.

When she was finished, Mrs. H said, "Jonathan, your grandmother told me you like to sing. Would you sing a song with me?"

The music in his heart said, "Yes!" so quickly it even surprised Jonathan.

"Do you know the song Twinkle Twinkle Little Star?" Jonathan nodded, and Mrs. H began to play.

As he started to sing, all Jonathan's sadness melted away, and his heart soared once again. Mrs. H said she would meet Jonathan to sing with him every day after school.

Every afternoon, as soon as the school bell rang, Jonathan ran to his grandmother's house, forgetting to be quiet and invisible.

One day, Mrs. H asked Jonathan if he would sing with her at the Strawberry Festival. He wanted to do it because she had been so nice to him. So, he agreed.

On the day of the festival, Jonathan looked in the mirror while he was getting ready. He still had sharp-looking quills, a long pointy nose, and beady eyes, but now, he also had a smile.

When it was time to sing, Jonathan saw the squirrels in the audience laughing and pointing at him. He started to leave when Mrs. H took his hand, and together they went on stage.

When the music started, Jonathan only felt the song in his heart, not the mean voices of the squirrels in the audience.

After the concert, many animals came up to Jonathan to say he was amazing. The squirrels were the ones being quiet now.

Jonathan was still different, but that was okay with him.

Jonathan the Boy

Sometimes the words come out of their mouth, and sometimes the words come out of their eyes. So, I just keep my head down. Even with my head down, I can feel the words hitting me and touching me and sticking to me. And so, the words become me. And I get very sad.

It's easier when I'm at home. At home, I don't have to worry about what other people see. I don't have to look in the mirror. I don't have to be anything but me. So, I'd rather stay home. But I can't. I have to go to school. I have to walk to school and feel the words stick to my back, stick to my legs, stick to my eyes, stick to my heart.

When I get to school, I don't have friends. I just sit there, and I wait, and I think, and I wait for the day to be over so that I can go home.

I like to sing. It helps me feel like I belong somewhere. It helps me feel like I have a place in the world. But school isn't always about singing. It's about belonging to things where you never belong. It's about math and science and words that hurt. I can feel comfortable at home. I can feel safe at home. Then I walk out the door, and the first person's words hit me. I'm ugly. I'm fat. I'm lazy. I'm slow. I'm a slob. The words hit me over and over and over until they become me.

I have a teacher who knows I can sing. That's the best part of my day, when I can go into the music room, and I don't feel words. The words fall off, and I sing. The words fall off me, and the music comes out, and there is a moment when I'm beautiful, when I'm happy, when I'm okay. I love the feeling of music surrounding me instead of words surrounding me. When things get to be too much, and I can't sing anymore, I think that will be the end.

I've thought about wanting to look like everybody else, wear skinny jeans, have my hair a certain way, wear the right clothes and the right shoes and the right everything. It seems like so much work. So, maybe they're right. Maybe I'm lazy, or maybe it's because that's not really who I am. It's what other people want me to look like. And I don't know how to do that. It's not working for me. It's never going to be what I look like or who I am.

I think if I had a friend, those things wouldn't be important. Those things wouldn't be the things they look for. They would look at me when I was singing. They would look at me when I was happy. They would realize that I'm a good friend. I'm very loyal. I'm funny. I think these things, and I think today, I'm going to make a friend. I walk out the door, and I feel good, and I don't look in a mirror, and I feel okay until people's words hit me. And then I remember, and I feel bad again.

Jonathan the Inspiration

Jonathan Antoine is a talented musician with an incredible singing voice. His story was told when he was a contestant on Britain's Got Talent in 2012, which helped start his career as a vocalist.

Jonathan says, "There's only one way to express what music gives me. It gives me purpose. It gives me point. When I sing, I can just be me." Jonathan credits his singing coach as one of the greatest influences of his young life.

Jonathan was bullied as a young child and became despondent at times. Music helped him find his place in the world. Jonathan wants children to know that they are not alone, and he hopes adults will help each child realize his or her potential.

Chelsea the Illustrator

Chelsea Rae Meeker is a 20 year-old college student, from Madrid, Iowa. Chelsea was diagnosed with Central Auditory Processing Disorder (CAPD), renamed Autism Spectrum Disorder (ASD), at age five. Her homeschool journey began after being told she could not learn in a classroom at the age of six.

At the age of 13, Chelsea discovered her love for art and began to dream that someday, she would write and illustrate children's books. Shortly after she was diagnosed with Hyperacusis, which made everything in the outside world painfully loud, she found her voice and comfort in her art.

After years of struggling with an invisible disability, a passion grew within her. She began using her special abilities to help others who also struggle with feeling invisible. What a blessing it has been to be part of such a beautiful project!

Cathie the Author

Cathie Gebhart is a retired schoolteacher, Momma to four, and Mema to four littles. During her career, she taught all grades from preschool to college. One of her greatest honors as a teacher was receiving the Rosa Parks Teaching Tolerance Award. She has many wonderful memories of her students and is proud to have been a part of their education.

Thank you to everyone who helped this series change from a possibility to a reality. Love and peace to all!

Made in the USA
Columbia, SC
26 February 2020